AF599247

THE PHILADELPHIA EAGLES

BY ALICIA Z. KLEPEIS

NFL ★ TEAM PROFILES

EPIC

BELLWETHER MEDIA ★ MINNEAPOLIS, MN

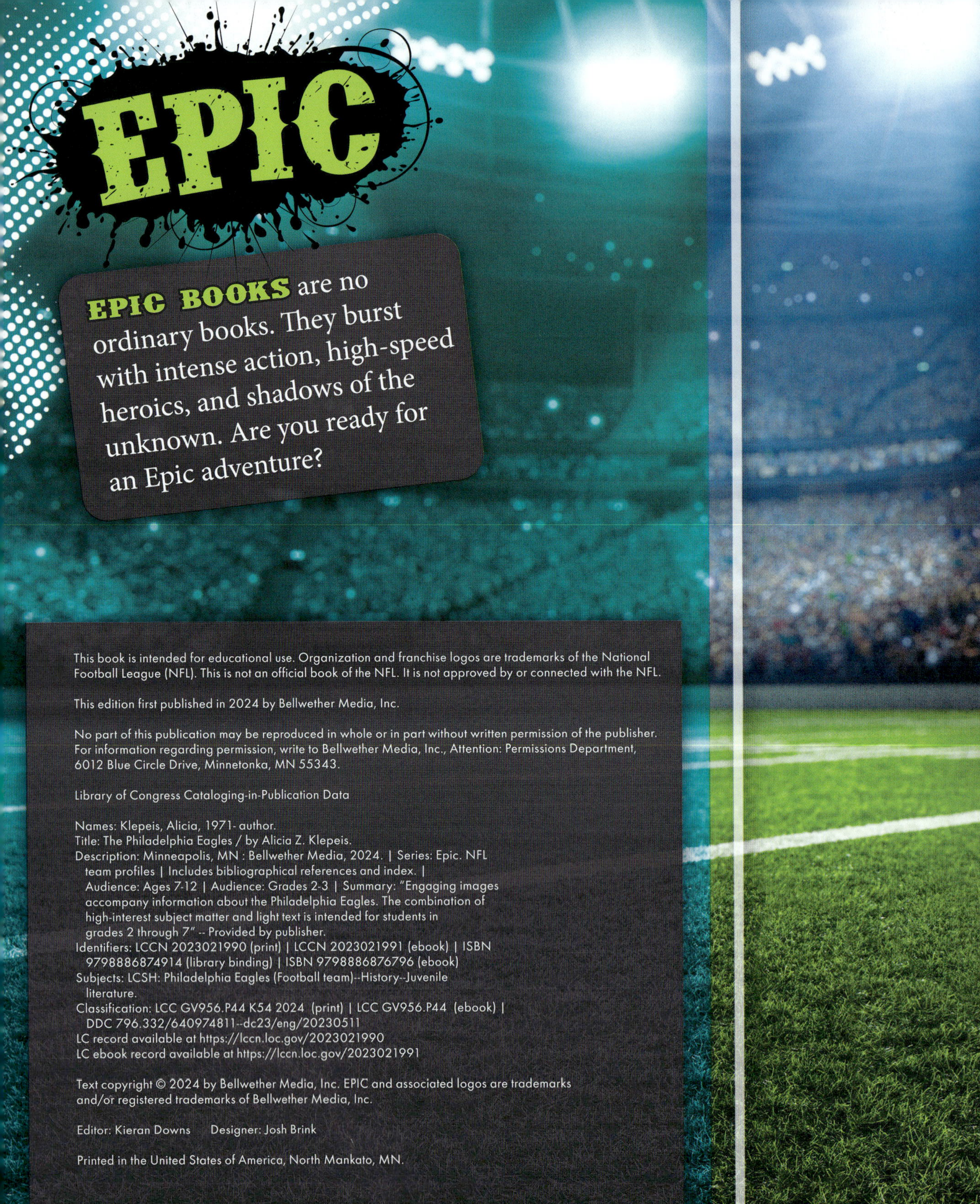

This edition first published in 2024 by Bellwether Media, Inc.

Library of Congress Cataloging-in-Publication Data

Names: Klepeis, Alicia, 1971- author.
Title: The Philadelphia Eagles / by Alicia Z. Klepeis.
Description: Minneapolis, MN : Bellwether Media, 2024. | Series: Epic. NFL team profiles | Includes bibliographical references and index. | Audience: Ages 7-12 | Audience: Grades 2-3 | Summary: "Engaging images accompany information about the Philadelphia Eagles. The combination of high-interest subject matter and light text is intended for students in grades 2 through 7" -- Provided by publisher.
Identifiers: LCCN 2023021990 (print) | LCCN 2023021991 (ebook) | ISBN 9798886874914 (library binding) | ISBN 9798886876796 (ebook)
Subjects: LCSH: Philadelphia Eagles (Football team)--History--Juvenile literature.
Classification: LCC GV956.P44 K54 2024 (print) | LCC GV956.P44 (ebook) | DDC 796.332/640974811--dc23/eng/20230511
LC record available at https://lccn.loc.gov/2023021990
LC ebook record available at https://lccn.loc.gov/2023021991

Editor: Kieran Downs Designer: Josh Brink

Printed in the United States of America, North Mankato, MN.

TABLE OF CONTENTS

THE PHILLY SPECIAL

TREY BURTON

The Eagles face the Patriots in **Super Bowl** 52. Eagles **running back** Corey Clement gets the ball. He flips it to **tight end** Trey Burton.

Burton passes to **quarterback** Nick Foles. **Touchdown**! The Eagles go on to win!

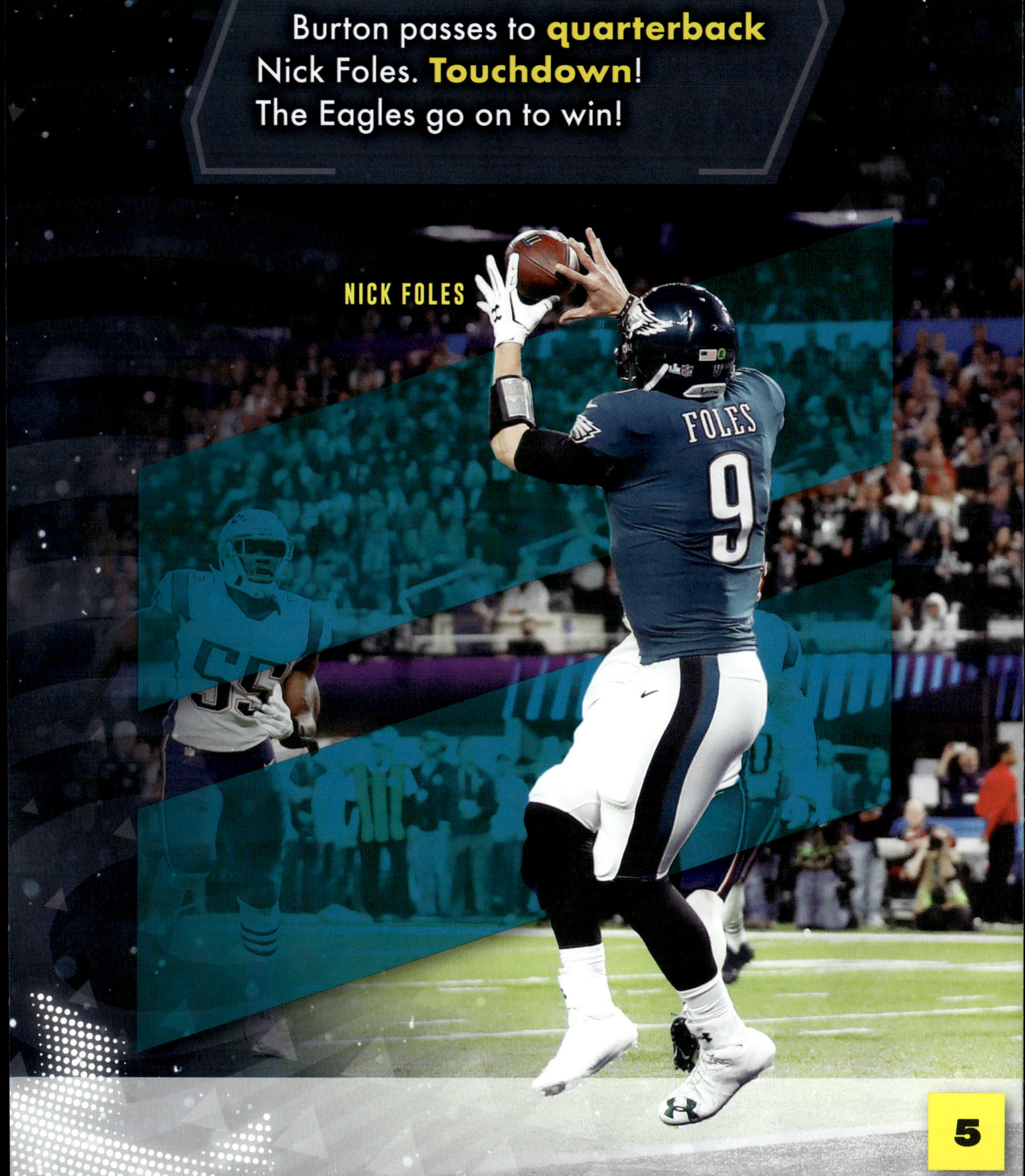

NICK FOLES

THE HISTORY OF THE EAGLES

The Eagles joined the National Football League (NFL) in 1933. The team struggled early on.

Coach Earle "Greasy" Neale turned things around in the 1940s. Running back Steve Van Buren helped. The team won the NFL **championship** in 1948 and 1949!

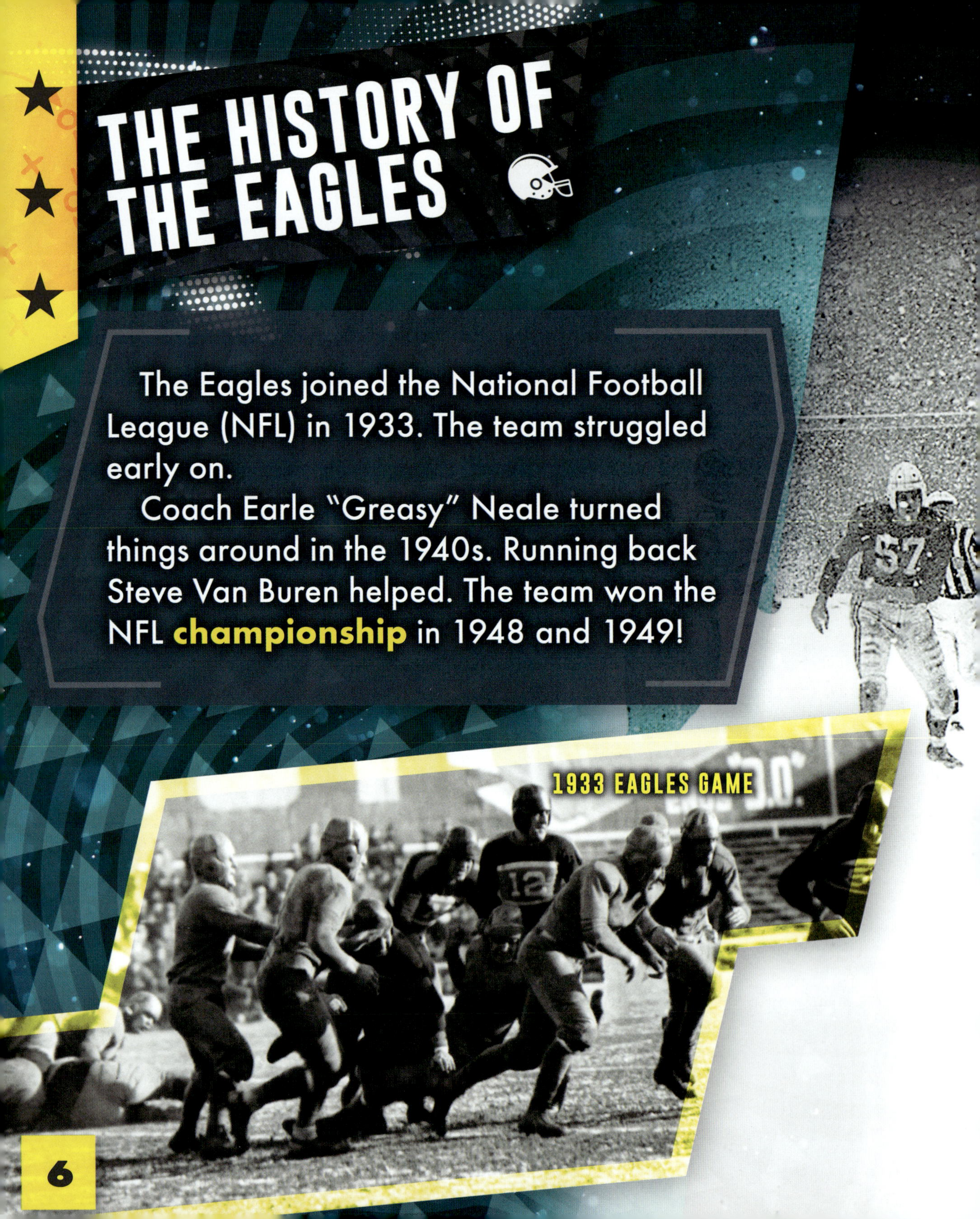

1933 EAGLES GAME

THE PHILLY SNOW

The 1948 NFL Championship Game took place in a snowstorm. Fans who came with shovels could watch for free! The Eagles beat the Chicago Cardinals 7–0.

1948 NFL CHAMPIONSHIP GAME

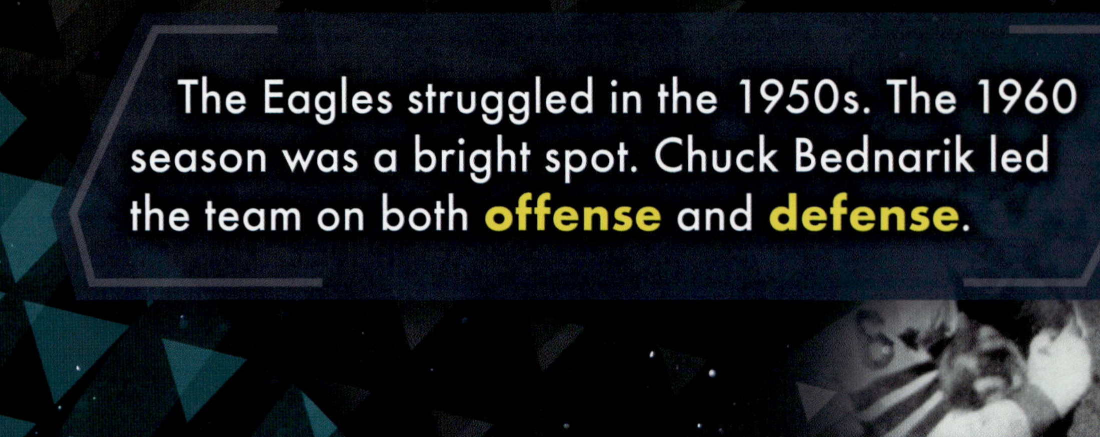

The Eagles struggled in the 1950s. The 1960 season was a bright spot. Chuck Bednarik led the team on both **offense** and **defense**.

1959 EAGLES GAME

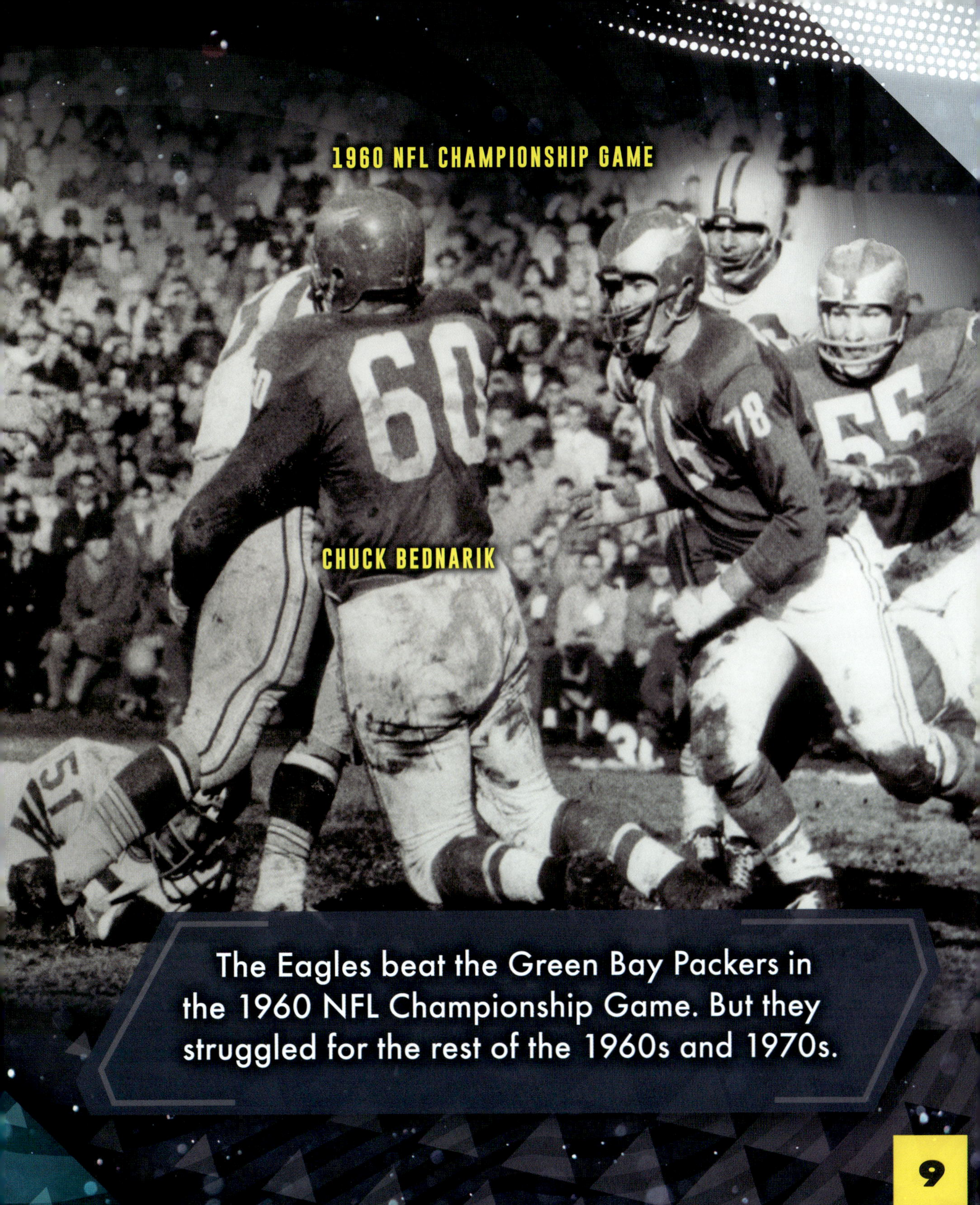

The Eagles beat the Green Bay Packers in the 1960 NFL Championship Game. But they struggled for the rest of the 1960s and 1970s.

The Eagles returned to the **playoffs** in 1978. In 1981, they reached the Super Bowl but lost.

SUPER BOWL 15

The Eagles made the playoffs eight times in the 1980s and 1990s. But they did not return to the Super Bowl.

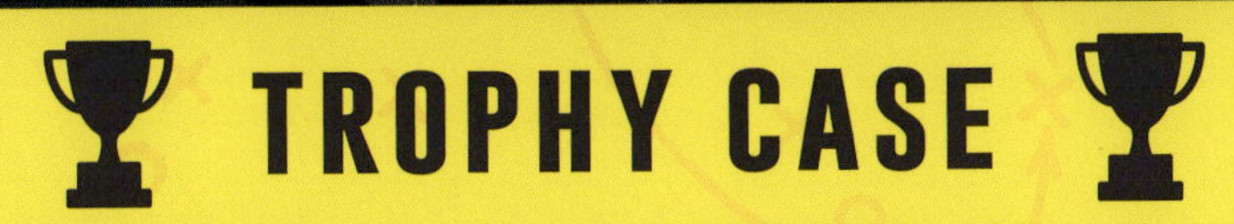

TROPHY CASE

NFC EAST championships 12

NFC championships 4

SUPER BOWL championships 1

NFL championships 3

In 2005, the Eagles returned to the Super Bowl. But they lost to the New England Patriots.

SUPER BOWL 39

In 2018, the team won their first Super Bowl! They won 41–33. The team returned to the Super Bowl in 2023. They lost to the Kansas City Chiefs.

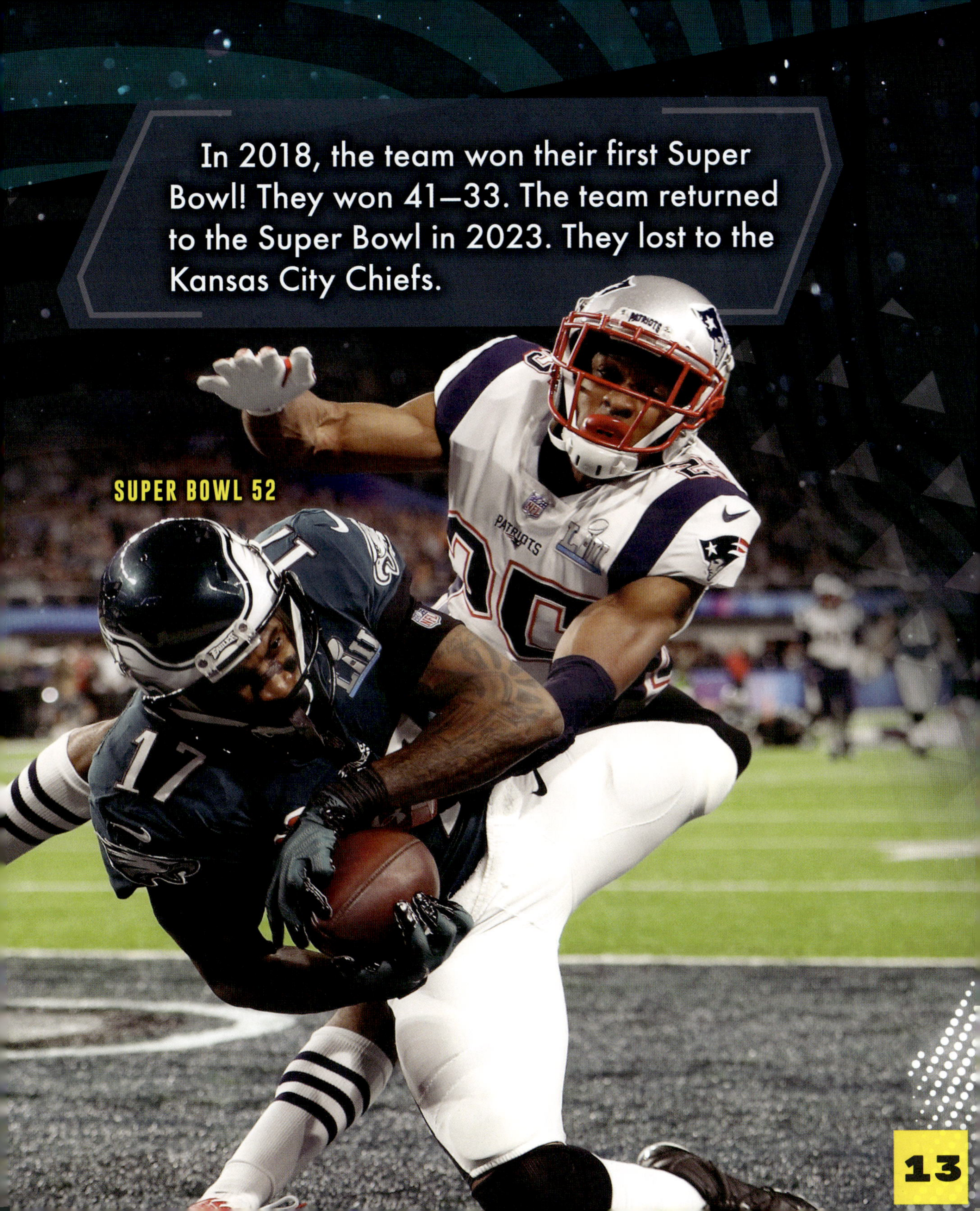

SUPER BOWL 52

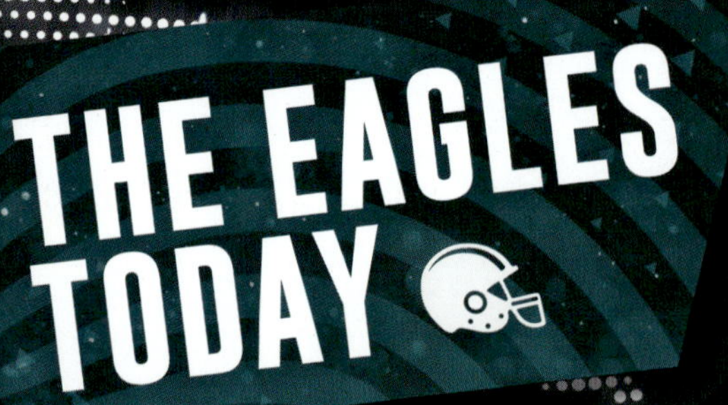

THE EAGLES TODAY

EAGLES VS. GIANTS

The Eagles play at Lincoln Financial Field. Fans call it the Linc. It is in Philadelphia, Pennsylvania.

The team plays in the NFC East. The New York Giants are one main **rival**. The Dallas Cowboys are another.

ONE HUGE PAINTING

Artists, Eagles fans, and players all worked to create a huge painting called "Our City, Our Team." It is located across from the Linc.

LOCATION

PENNSYLVANIA

N
W E
S

LINCOLN FINANCIAL FIELD

Philadelphia, Pennsylvania

GAME DAY!

The Eagles' **mascot** is Swoop. He cheers and greets fans on game days.

Fans dress in the team colors. They are midnight green, silver, black, and white. Some fans wear eagle masks or fake wings.

SWOOP

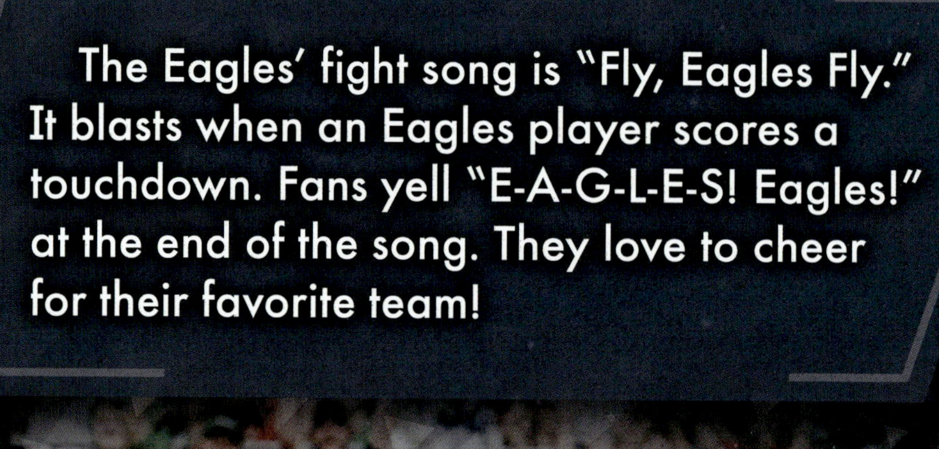

The Eagles' fight song is "Fly, Eagles Fly." It blasts when an Eagles player scores a touchdown. Fans yell "E-A-G-L-E-S! Eagles!" at the end of the song. They love to cheer for their favorite team!

★ FAMOUS PLAYERS ★

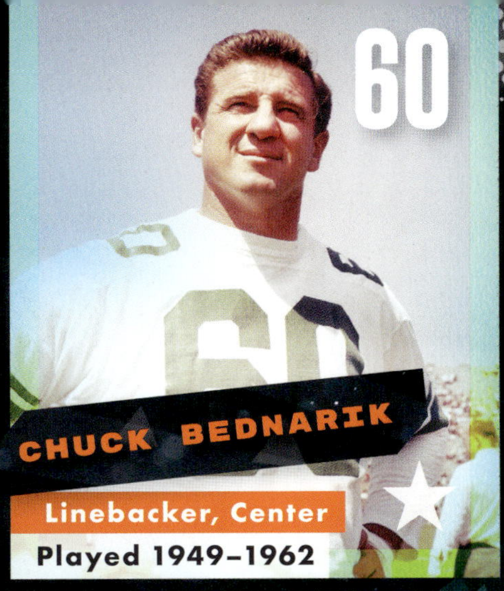

CHUCK BEDNARIK

Linebacker, Center

Played 1949–1962

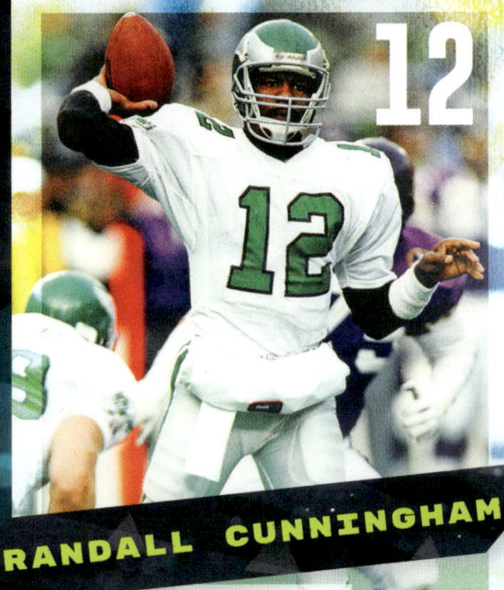

RANDALL CUNNINGHAM

Quarterback

Played 1985–1995

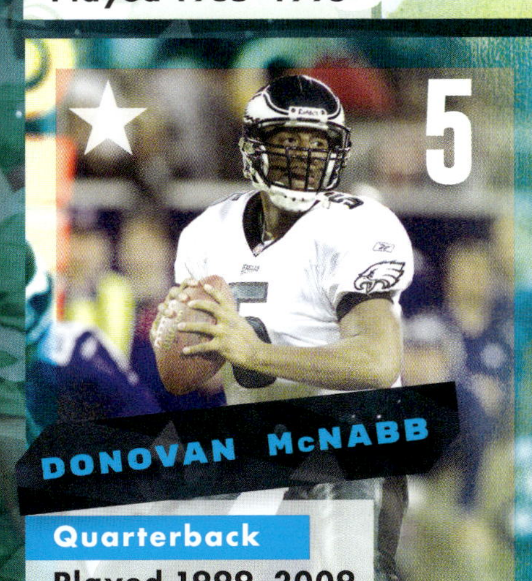

DONOVAN McNABB

Quarterback

Played 1999–2009

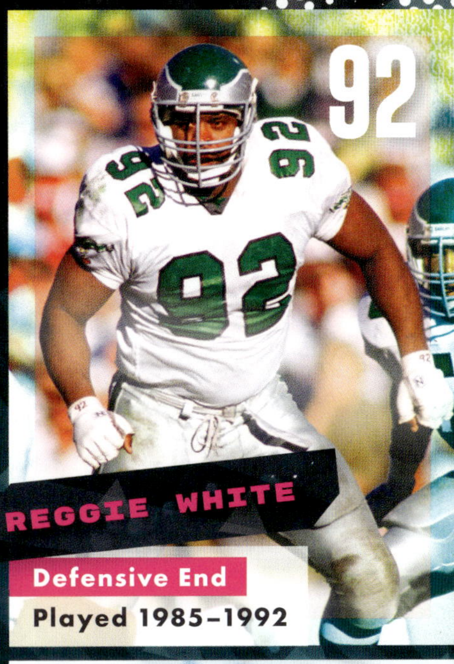

REGGIE WHITE

Defensive End

Played 1985–1992

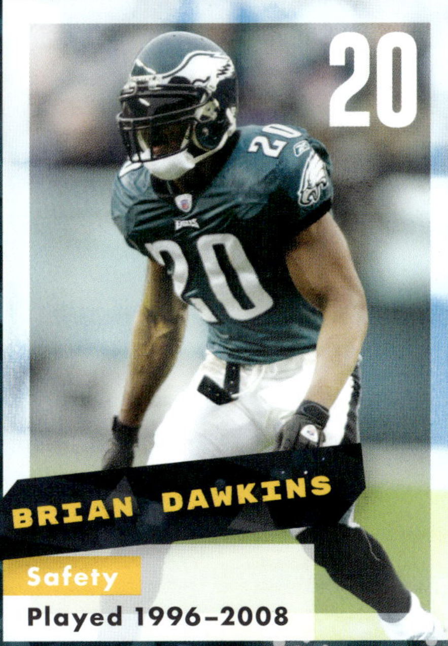

BRIAN DAWKINS

Safety

Played 1996–2008

PHILADELPHIA EAGLES FACTS

LOGO

JOINED THE NFL | 1933

NICKNAMES | The Birds, The Iggles

MASCOT

SWOOP

CONFERENCE

National Football Conference (NFC)

COLORS

DIVISION | NFC East

Dallas Cowboys

New York Giants

Washington Commanders

STADIUM

LINCOLN FINANCIAL FIELD

opened August 3, 2003

holds 67,594 people

TIMELINE

1933
The Eagles play their first season in the NFL

1960
The Eagles win the NFL championship

1981
The Eagles play in their first Super Bowl

2018
The Eagles win Super Bowl 52

2023
The Eagles play in Super Bowl 57

RECORDS

All-Time Passing Leader
Donovan McNabb
32,873 yards

All-Time Receiving Leader
Harold Carmichael
8,978 yards

All-Time Rushing Leader
LeSean McCoy
6,792 yards

All-Time Scoring Leader
David Akers
1,323 points

GLOSSARY

championship—a contest to decide the best team or person

defense—the group of players who try to stop the opposing team from scoring

mascot—an animal or symbol that represents a sports team

offense—the group of players who have the ball and try to score

playoffs—games played after the regular season is over; playoff games determine which teams play in the championship game.

quarterback—a player whose main job is to throw and hand off the ball

rival—a long-standing opponent

running back—a player whose main job is to run with the ball

Super Bowl—the annual championship game of the NFL

tight end—a player whose main jobs are to catch the ball and block for teammates

touchdown—a score that occurs when a team crosses into their opponent's end zone with the football; a touchdown is worth six points.

AT THE LIBRARY

Coleman, Ted. *Philadelphia Eagles.* Mendota Heights, Minn.: Press Room Editions, 2021.

Cooper, Robert. *Philadelphia Eagles.* Minneapolis, Minn.: ABDO Publishing, 2020.

Goodman, Michael E. *Philadelphia Eagles.* Mankato, Minn.: Creative Education, 2023.

ON THE WEB

FACTSURFER

Factsurfer.com gives you a safe, fun way to find more information.

1. Go to www.factsurfer.com.
2. Enter "Philadelphia Eagles" into the search box and click 🔍.
3. Select your book cover to see a list of related content.

INDEX

The images in this book are reproduced through the courtesy of: Matt Slocum/ AP Images, cover (hero); Brian E Kushner, cover (stadium); All-Pro Reels/ Wikipedia, p. 3; Perry Knotts/ AP Images, pp. 4-5; Jeff Roberson/ AP Images, p. 5; ASSOCIATED PRESS/ AP Images, pp. 6, 6-7, 8, 21 (1933, 1960); BEVER/ AP Images, pp. 9-10; Focus On Sport/ Getty, pp. 10-11, 21 (1981, Harold Carmichael); Jeff Gross/ Getty, p. 12; Patrick Smith/ Getty, pp. 13, 21 (2018); Scott Serio/ AP Images, p. 14; Brian E Kushner, p. 15; NFL/ Wikipedia, p. 15 (Eagles logo), p. 20 (Eagles logo, Cowboys logo, Giants logo, Commanders logo, NFC logo); Scott Taetsch/ Getty, p. 16; Christopher Polk/ Getty, pp. 16-17; The Washington Post/ Getty, pp. 18-19; DUROD/ AP Images, p. 19 (Chuck Bednarik, Reggie White); PACET/ AP Images, p. 19 (Randall Cunningham); BOEHS/ AP Images, p. 19 (Brian Dawkins); Jamie Squire/ Getty, p. 19 (Donovan McNabb); Icon Sportswire/ Getty, p. 20 (mascot); Brian Kushner/ Alamy, p. 20 (stadium); Ezra Shaw/ Getty, p. 21 (2023); M. David Leeds/ Getty, p. 21 (Donovan McNabb); Rob Tringali/ Sportschrome/ Getty, p. 21 (LeSean McCoy); Al Bello/ Getty, p. 21 (David Akers); Cal Sport Media/ Alamy, p. 23.